This journal belongs to

Made in the USA
Middletown, DE
22 February 2022

61664705R00084